BENEDETTA

MIRALLES

TAGLIABUE

ENRIC

EMBT Arquitectes

720. 9̶2̶ MIR

720 MIR

This book is due for return on or before the last date shown below.

WITHDRAWN

3.99

# EMBT Arquitectes

**teNeues**

**Editor in chief:**
Paco Asensio

**Editor and original texts:**
Aurora Cuito

**English translation:**
William Bain

**German translation:**
Martin Fischer

**French translation:**
Agencia Lingo Sense

**Italian translation:**
Grazia Sufritti

**Art direction:**
Mireia Casanovas Soley

**Graphic Design / Layout:**
Emma Termes Parera and Soti Mas-Bagà


**Published worldwide by teNeues Publishing Group**
(except Spain, Portugal and South-America):

**teNeues Book Division**
Kaistraße 18, 40221 Düsseldorf, Germany
Tel.: 0049-(0)211-994597-0
Fax: 0049-(0)211-994597-40

**teNeues Publishing Company**
16 West 22nd Street, New York, N.Y., 10010, USA
Tel.: 001-212-627-9090
Fax: 001-212-627-9511

**teNeues Publishing UK Ltd.**
P.O. Box 402
West Byfleet
KT14 7ZF
Tel.: 0044-1932-403509
Fax: 0044-1932-403514

**teNeues France S.A.R.L.**
140, rue de la Croix Nivert
75015 Paris, France
Tel.: 0033-1-5576-6205
Fax: 0033-1-5576-6419


**www.teneues.com**


**Editorial project:**

© 2003 **LOFT** Publications
Via Laietana, 32 4° Of. 92
08003 Barcelona, Spain
Tel.: 0034 932 688 088
Fax: 0034 932 687 073
e-mail: loft@loftpublications.com
www.loftpublications.com

**Printed by:**
Anman Gràfiques del Vallès, Spain
June 2003

Bibliographic information published by Die Deutsche Bibliothek
Die Deutsche Bibliothek lists this publication in the Deutsche
Nationalbibliografie; detailed bibliographic data is available in the
Internet at http://dnb.ddb.de.

ISBN: 3-8238-4540-3

We would like to show sincere gratefulness to the office of EMBT
Arquitectes, specially to Isabel Zaragoza for her useful collaboration.

In looking at the work of Enric Miralles and Benedetta Tagliabue, the viewer instinctively perceives that time has been factored in as one more material. This is true not only in speaking of the temporal as a dimension that ages and deteriorates buildings but also as something that is an integral part of the project, like bricks, say, or steel, or concrete. This sensitivity makes EMBT buildings fragments in a story, the story of that building's users and of its surroundings.

In a given time, and in a given city, Barcelona, where architects have always aimed at preserving the cultural identity via mimetic and repetitive gestures, EMBT's trajectory stands out by way of employing a unique language. This is avant-garde, this is daring, this, for some, is in-your-face discourse, yet it is also tremendously respectful of the context. In not employing regional or vernacular architectural paradigms, the company has unchained a radical and passionate interpretation of modernity.

The expertise and talent of Miralles and Tagliabue shows through every one of the projects that bear the name of their office. This is as true of the new pieces as it is of the structures like the Gas Natural tower or the parks in Mollet del Vallès and Diagonal Mar. It is true, however, above all in the interventions that conflate new and old, as in the house on the calle Mercaders, the rehabilitation of the Santa Caterina Market, or the new headquarters of the Istituto Universitario di Architettura di Venezia.

Wer die Werke von Enric Miralles und Benedetta Tagliabue betrachtet, nimmt instinktiv wahr, dass die Zeit dort wie ein weiterer Werkstoff eingesetzt wird. Sie erscheint nicht nur als eine Dimension, die sich im Alterungsprozess des Gebäudes offenbart, sondern als ein integraler Bestandteil des Entwurfs, ebenso wie Backstein, Stahl oder Beton. Diese Sensibilität lässt die Bauten des Büros EMBT zu Elementen einer Geschichte werden, der Geschichte ihrer Nutzer und des Umfelds.

In der heutigen Zeit und in Barcelona als einer Stadt, in der die Architekten stets darauf bedacht waren, mittels Wiederholungen und Nachahmungen die kulturelle Eigenart zu bewahren, treten EMBT durch ihre eigene gewagte, zuweilen fast unverschämte avantgardistische Sprache hervor, die jedoch äußerst behutsam mit dem Umfeld umgeht. Die Architekten lehnen regionale oder ortsübliche Vorbilder ab und treten für eine radikale, leidenschaftliche Auslegung der Moderne ein.

Der Sachverstand und das Talent von Miralles und Tagliabue kommen in allen Projekten des Büros zum Ausdruck, in den Neubauten wie dem Hochhaus für Gas Natural oder den Parks in Mollet del Vallès und Diagonal Mar, vor allem jedoch in den Umbauten oder Erweiterungen, bei denen alt und neu miteinander vermengt werden, wie im Haus in der Mercaders Straße, bei der Neugestaltung des Marktes Santa Caterina oder dem neuen Sitz des Istituto Universitario di Architettura di Venezia.

En observant l'œuvre d'Enric Miralles et de Benedetta Tagliabue, le spectateur perçoit instinctivement que le temps a été traité comme un matériau de plus. Non comme une dimension vieillissant les constructions et les détériorant mais bien comme une partie intégrante du projet, ainsi les briques, l'acier ou le béton. Cette sensibilité convertit les constructions d'EMBT en fragments d'une histoire, celle de leurs usagers et de l'environnement.

À une époque et dans une ville, Barcelone, où les architectes ont toujours souhaité préserver l'identité culturelle par des gestes mimétiques et répétitifs, le parcours d'EMBT se distingue par l'emploi d'un langage propre, avant-gardiste, osé et, pour certains, effronté mais aussi superbement respectueux du contexte. En renonçant aux modèles architecturaux régionaux ou vernaculaires, il a généré une interprétation radicale et passionnée de la modernité.

L'expertise et le talent de Miralles et Tagliabue sont matérialisées dans chaque œuvre du cabinet : qu'il s'agisse des nouvelles réalisations comme la tour Gas Natural ou des parcs de Mollet del Vallès et de Diagonal Mar, mais aussi et surtout des interventions où se mêlent le nouveau et l'ancien, ainsi la maison de la rue Mercaders, la réhabilitation du marché de Santa Caterina o enfin du nouveau siège de l'Istituto Universitario di Architettura di Venezia.

Osservando l'opera di Enric Miralles e Benedetta Tagliabue, lo spettatore percepisce istintivamente che il tempo è stato trattato come un materiale in più, non solo come una dimensione che invecchia le costruzioni e le deteriora, ma che piuttosto forma parte integrante del progetto, come i mattoni, l'acciaio o il cemento. Questa sensibilità trasforma gli edifici di EMBT in frammenti di una storia, quella dei suoi utenti e quella del suo ambiente.

In un'epoca ed in una città, quella di Barcellona, dove gli architetti hanno voluto salvaguardare l'identità culturale mediante gesti mimetici e ripetitivi, la traiettoria di EMBT si distingue per utilizzare un linguaggio proprio, avanguardista, coraggioso e, per alcuni, quasi sfacciato, ma anche tremendamente attento al contesto. Il rinunciare a modelli architettonici regionali o locali ha generato un'interpretazione radicale e appassionata della modernità.

La perizia ed il talento di Miralles e Tagliabue hanno preso forma in tutti i lavori dello studio, sia nelle nuove opere, come la torre della sede della compagnia del Gas Natural o i parchi di Mollet del Vallès e Diagonal Mar, ma soprattutto negli interventi dove si fondono il nuovo e l'antico, come nella casa di via Mercaders, il restauro del mercato di Santa Caterina o la nuova sede dell'Istituto Universitario di Architettura di Venezia.

# House in Mercaders Street

Location: Mercaders, Barcelona, Spain
Date of construction: 1993–1994
Photographer: Duccio Malagamba

**More than any other building, the house of an architect is a faithful reflection of his language, his desires, his worries—definitively, of his style. The house of Enric Miralles and Benedetta Tagliabue is a veritable laboratory of experimentation in this regard: it shows a wide repertory of gestures and solutions, both constructive and conceptual. And these are things that have been developed in most of their projects. The house in question, in the center of Barcelona, occupies part of a Gothic palace, with independent entranceway and garden. The intervention was centered on the discovery of the building's original elements so as to keep them in the new house. And Gothic arches, fragments of frescoes on the walls, and a floor of ceramic tiles were found. The interior, which was much deteriorated, didn't have a single vertical plane left standing. Thus, the beginning of the project brought the idea of dividing the space with curtains. The required functionality made these into movable pieces of furniture, wooden doors in some cases, screens in others. The aforementioned tiles were kept for flooring in front of the windows and, on occasion, were combined with wood in the walls.**

In keinem anderen Werk kommen seine Formensprache, seine Vorlieben, seine Bestrebungen, kurz gesagt, sein Stil besser zum Ausdruck als im Haus eines Architekten. So stellt sich auch das Haus von Enric Miralles und Benedetta Tagliabue als ein wahres Experimentierfeld mit einem reichhaltigen Repertoire konstruktiver und gestalterischer Lösungen dar. Viele der hier erkennbaren Ansätze entwickelten die Architekten in ihren anderen Projekten weiter. Das Wohnhaus nimmt Teile eines gotischen Stadtpalais im Zentrum von Barcelona ein und verfügt über einen eigenen Eingang und einen Garten. Zunächst ging es darum, originale Bauelemente aufzufinden, um sie beim Ausbau verwenden zu können. Zum Vorschein kamen gotische Bögen, Reste von Fresken an den Wänden und der ehemalige Fußboden aus Terrakottafliesen. Das Innere war in einem sehr schlechten Zustand, es gab keine senkrechten Unterteilungen mehr, sodass man erst daran dachte, den Raum nur mit Vorhängen zu unterteilen. Aus funktionalen Erwägungen wurden dann allerdings Möbel, Holztüren und leichte Trennwände als Raumteiler eingesetzt. Die Tonfliesen fanden im Fußboden vor den Fenstern Verwendung und wurden teilweise auch mit Holz kombiniert an den Wänden wieder verwendet.

Mieux que quelque autre œuvre, la maison d'un architecte est le reflet fidèle de son langage, de ses appétits, de ses inquiétudes et, en définitive, de son style. La maison d'Enric Miralles et Benedetta Tagliabue est un véritable champ d'expérimentation et dévoile un ample répertoire de gestes et de solutions pratiques ou conceptuelles, développées pour d'autres projets. La demeure, située au centre de Barcelone, occupe une partie d'un palais gothique, avec entrée et jardin indépendants. L'intervention s'est centrée sur la découverte d'éléments originels afin qu'ils fassent partie de la nouvelle maison ; ont été révélés des arches gothiques, des fragments de fresque aux murs et un revêtement en céramiques. L'intérieur, très détérioré, ne présentait aucune partition verticale, la division de l'espace par des rideaux avait ainsi été retenue dans un premier temps. La nécessaire fonctionnalité a converti ces partitions en meubles mobiles, portes de bois et cloisons. Les céramiques ont été utilisées au sol devant les fenêtre et, parfois, mêlées au bois sur les murs.

Più di qualsiasi altra opera, la casa di un architetto è il fedele riflesso del suo linguaggio, dei suoi desideri, delle sue inquietudini e, in definitiva, del suo stile. La casa di Enric Miralles e Benedetta Tagliabue è un vero spazio sperimentale e mostra un ampio repertorio dei gesti e delle soluzioni, sia costruttive che concettuali, che i due hanno sviluppato in altri progetti. La casa, situata nel centro di Barcellona, occupa parte di un palazzo gotico, con entrata e giardino indipendenti. L'intervento è stato centrato nell'individuare gli elementi originali perché formassero parte della nuova casa; sono stati scoperti archi gotici, frammenti di affreschi alle pareti ed un pavimento di formelle di ceramica. L'interno, assai deteriorato, non presentava nessuna divisoria verticale, per cui all'inizio fu considerata la possibilità di dividere lo spazio con delle tende. La necessaria funzionalità ha trasformato queste partizioni in mobili scorrevoli, porte di legno ed alcune tramezzature. Le piastrelle sono state utilizzate come pavimento davanti alle finestre ed in alcuni casi sono state utilizzate insieme al legno nelle pareti.

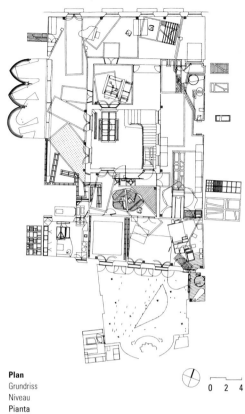

**Plan**
Grundriss
Niveau
**Pianta**

0 2 4

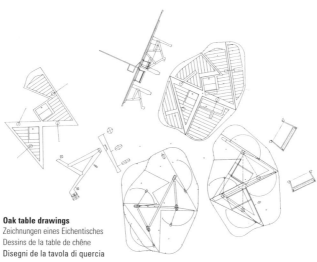

**Oak table drawings**
Zeichnungen eines Eichentisches
Dessins de la table de chêne
Disegni de la tavola di quercia

# House in La Clota

Location: Barcelona, Spain
Date of construction: 1998
Photographer: Jordi Miralles

**This project is the result of joining two pre-existing buildings in the Barcelona neighborhood of La Clota. The aim of the work was to restore and extend both houses, which were divided by party walls. Both residences were two-story affairs and the plan from the outset was to convert them into a single residence with a studio-library as mainspring. The architects preserved the general structure of one of the houses, including the access stairway to the upper level, although part of the floors were cleared. In the ground floor, the domestic program was developed: a living room and dining room, with the kitchen at the back; and in the first floor the assembly of three bedrooms. More dramatic action was taken next door: the rooms were largely gutted and on the last level of the building a catwalk and lantern were constructed. This last element, suspended from the roof, bathes the new building in overhead natural light. The walls, painted in white, and the flooring, based on cuts of different types of wood, reinforce the diffuse illumination.**

Der Bauherr wollte zwei Häuser im Viertel La Clota von Barcelona miteinander verbinden. Es handelt sich um zwei nebeneinander liegende zweigeschossige Altbauten, die restauriert und erweitert wurden, um eine großzügige Bibliothek unterzubringen. Bei dem einen der beiden Häuser blieb während des Ausbaus die Struktur weitgehend erhalten. Auch die Treppe vom Erdgeschoss in den ersten Stock wurde übernommen. Allerdings erfolgten stellenweise Eingriffe bei den Stockwerken. In diesem Haus befinden sich die eigentlichen Wohnräume: Wohnzimmer, Esszimmer und Küche im Erdgeschoss, im ersten Stock drei Schlafzimmer. Im anderen Haus wurden drastischere Veränderungen vorgenommen: Sowohl im Dach als auch in der Zwischendecke wurden Durchbrüche geschaffen und es wurde eine umlaufende Galerie eingebaut. Das Innere erhält durch das außergewöhnliche Oberlicht reichlich natürliches Licht, das durch die weißen Wände noch verstärkt wird und den aus verschiedenen Hölzern gestalteten Fußboden besonders gut zur Geltung bringt.

Ce projet est le résultat de l'unification de deux édifices préexistants du quartier barcelonais de La Clota. L'œuvre avait pour objet la restauration et l'ampliation des deux maisons, entre des murs mitoyens et présentant chacune deux étages, afin de les convertir en une demeure unique dont la bibliothèque et l'étude seront les pièces significatives. L'intervention a conservé la structure générale de l'un des immeubles, incluant l'escalier d'accès au niveau supérieur, bien que la poutraison ait été vidée de certaines pièces. Cette zone a vu le développement du programme domestique : au rez-de-chaussée, le séjour, la salle à manger et la cuisine au fond ; en haut, les trois chambres. L'intervention dans l'autre immeuble fut plus drastique : la structure et la toiture du centre de l'étage ont été partiellement vidées et une passerelle et un lucernaire introduits. Cet élément, suspendu du toit, permet l'entrée d'une abondance de lumière zénithale, inondant l'intérieur. La peinture blanche et un revêtement à base de coupes de diverses essence de bois renforcent cette luminosité.

Questo progetto è il risultato della fusione di due costruzioni preesistenti nel quartiere La Clota di Barcellona. Lo scopo dell'intervento era il restauro e l'ampliamento delle due case – separate da divisorie e ciascuna di due piani – per trasformarle in un alloggio unico, con uno studio biblioteca come elemento significativo. L'intervento ha mantenuto la struttura generale di uno degli immobili, inclusa la scala d'accesso al piano superiore, anche se ha demolito i solai di alcune stanze. Questa zona è stata destinata all'uso domestico: al piano terra si trovano il soggiorno, il pranzo e la cucina al fondo; e al piano di sopra tre camere. L'intervento nell'altro alloggio è stato drastico: sono stati parzialmente demoliti il solaio e la copertura nella parte centrale e sono stati realizzati una passerella ed un lucernario. Quest'elemento, sospeso al tetto, permette l'entrata di abbondante luce zenitale. La tinteggiatura bianca ed un pavimento fatto di ritagli di diversi legnami ne rafforzano la luminosità.

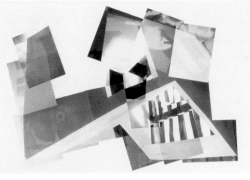

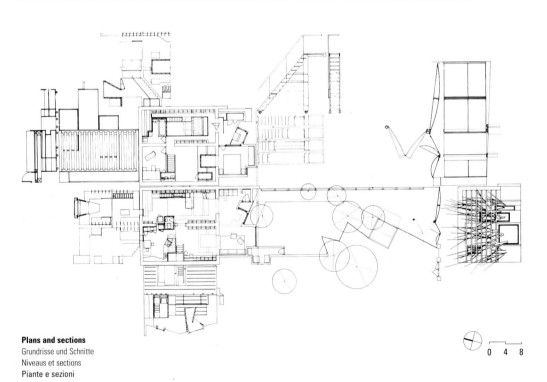

**Plans and sections**
Grundrisse und Schnitte
Niveaus et sections
Piante e sezioni

0  4  8

# School of Music

Location: Feldstraße 66, Hamburg, Germany
Collaborators: NPS + Partner Architekten BDA
Date of construction: 1997–2000
Photographer: Duccio Malagamba

One of the main aims was to create a building that harmonizes with its environment, marked by the neighboring structures and by the lushness of the woodland around the site itself. Therefore, the edifice was slotted among the trees and a series of resources was used to point up the presence of the vegetation: views from the woods were highlighted, columns miming tree trunks became part of the metaphor in the street façade. The children's energy in and out of class and the ways of channeling it has gone into classroom design. This vitality is present in the colors used in the planes of the building: in some cases it is used over metal panels with colors such as orange, yellow or green; in other cases the combination of courses of red brick with ochre brick. The school is organized into two large zones: the public area, which includes the accessways and the cafeteria; and the private area, which has the administration offices, the teachers' room, and the classrooms. The two areas share an entrance that can also be used separately when necessary.

Es ging vor allem darum, ein Gebäude zu schaffen, das sich in eine Umgebung einfügt, die gekennzeichnet ist durch die benachbarten Bauten und den dichten Baumbestand des Grundstücks. Das Gebäude steht dementsprechend inmitten von Bäumen und die Natur ist auch sonst immer präsent. Umgekehrt gewähren die großen Fenster auch Einblicke ins Innere des Gebäudes. Vor der Straßenfassade wurden Pfeiler aufgestellt, die als Metapher für die Baumstämme im Garten zu verstehen sind. Ein weiteres, die Entwurfsplanung bestimmendes Kriterium war es, die Energie der Kinder darzustellen, die die Klassenräume mit Leben erfüllen. Diese Lebenskraft kommt in der Farbgebung der Fassaden zum Ausdruck: Einige wurden mit orangefarbenen, gelben, grünen und andersfarbigen Metallpaneelen verkleidet, bei anderen findet man abwechselnd rötlichen und ockerfarbenen Backstein. Die Schule ist in zwei große Bereiche unterteilt: den öffentlichen mit der Eingangshalle und der Cafeteria und den eigentlichen Schulbereich mit den Klassenräumen, dem Lehrerzimmer und den Verwaltungsräumen. Der gemeinsame Zugang für beide Bereiche kann bei Bedarf auch unabhängig voneinander benutzt werden.

L'un des objectifs essentiels était de créer un bâtiment en harmonie avec son environnement, marqué par les constructions voisines et les frondaisons du bois accueillant le terrain. L'édifice a donc été situé parmi les arbres et diverses ressources ont été employées pour souligner la présence de la végétation, ainsi l'introduction de vues de l'extérieur à l'intérieur à l'aide de nombreuses fenêtres ou la disposition de piliers en une métaphore de troncs pour la structure de la façade donnant sur la rue. Un autre défi visait à exprimer l'énergie des enfants donnant vie aux salles de cours. Cette vitalité est matérialisée en usant de la couleur sur les façades : certaines ont été revêtues de panneaux métalliques aux tons orange, jaune, vert…, d'autres combinent les briques rougeâtres et ocre. L'école est organisée en deux grandes zones : la partie publique inclut les entrées et la caféféria ; la partie privée accueille les bureaux administratifs, la salle des professeurs et les salles de cours. Chaque partie partage un accès qui peut aussi être utilisé séparément, le cas échéant.

Uno dei principali obiettivi del progetto era quello di creare un edificio coerente con l'ambiente circostante, marcato dalle costruzioni contigue e dalla frondosità del bosco nel quale si trova il lotto. Così l'edificio è stato collocato tra gli alberi e sono stati impiegati diversi sistemi per enfatizzare la presenza della vegetazione, come ad esempio introdurre i paesaggi all'interno della scuola attraverso le numerose vetrate o collocare dei pilastri che rappresentano metaforicamente dei tronchi d'albero nella struttura della facciata che dà alla strada. Un'altra delle sfide era quella di cercare di esprimere l'energia dei bambini che danno vita a queste aule. Questa vitalità ha preso forma attraverso l'uso del colore nelle facciate: alcune sono state rivestite con pannelli metallici dai toni arancio, giallo, verde… altre alternano file di mattoni rossicci e color ocra. La scuola è organizzata in due grandi zone: quella pubblica, che include gli ingressi ed il bar; e quella privata, che accoglie gli uffici dell'amministrazione, la sala insegnanti e le aule. Le due parti condividono un accesso che, se necessario, può essere utilizzato separatamente.

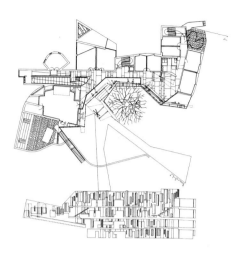

**First floor and section**
Erstes Obergeschoss und Schnitt
Premier étage et section
Piano primo e sezione

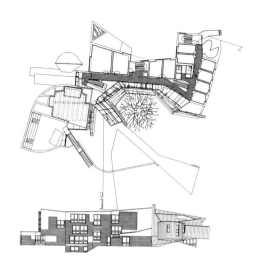

**Second floor and elevation**
Zweites Obergeschoss und Aufriss
Deuxième étage et élevation
Piano secondo e prospetto

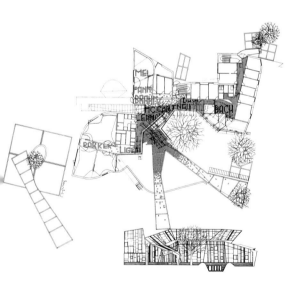

**Ground floor and section**
Erdgeschoss und Schnitt
Rez-de-chaussée et section
Piano terra e sezione

0  5  10

# Utrecht Town Hall

Location: Ganzenmarktstraat, Utrecht, Netherlands
Date of construction: 1999
Photographer: Duccio Malagamba

This commission was to enlarge the Town Hall of Utrecht, which no longer met the needs of a larger operation and could also benefit from the technical advances necessary for an official entity. From the outset the aim of the EMBT Studio involved a rediscovery of the value of interior spaces in the neoclassical building that was already standing. This was perhaps especially true of the medieval room, which had already been previously rehabilitated at different times. On the other hand, the architects wanted to go back to the idea of a municipal edifice as a conglomerate of different city structures which agglutinated different styles and materials as a reflection of the diversity of building arts in the Dutch town. To bring this into being, the work recycled materials like bricks and jambs and lintels of stone that came from the demolition of parts of the extant building. Owing, however, to the functional complexity involved, a redistribution of the activities was decided and the ground floor became a weave of public spaces on the model of a covered urban network while the first floor housed the political offices.

Der Entwurf sah die Erweiterung des alten Rathauses von Utrecht vor, das zu klein geworden war und außerdem den neuesten technischen Anforderungen, die an ein öffentliches Gebäude gestellt werden, nicht mehr genügte. Dem Büro EMBT war von Anfang an daran gelegen, den Wert der Innenräume des klassizistischen Altbaus wiederzuentdecken; das galt natürlich besonders für den mittelalterlichen Saal, der mehrmals umgestaltet worden war. Auf der anderen Seite stellten sich die Architekten das Rathaus als ein Konglomerat verschiedener Häuser der Stadt vor, das verschiedene Stile und Materialien in sich vereint und damit die Vielfältigkeit des Baugeschehens in dieser holländischen Stadt widerspiegelt. Deshalb wurden bei der Erweiterung Materialien und Bauteile wieder verwertet, die beim Abbruch einiger Teile des Altbaus angefallen waren, z.B. Backsteine sowie Fensterwandungen und Türstürze aus Stein. Aus funktionalen Erwägungen wurden im Erdgeschoss die öffentlichen Dienstleistungen umverteilt und wie in einer Art überdachter kleiner Stadt untergebracht, während im Obergeschoss die politischen Repräsentationsräume liegen.

Cette commande avait pour objet l'agrandissement de l'Hôtel de ville d'Utrecht, désormais à l'étroit dans ses murs et en retard techniquement par rapport à son rôle d'organisme officiel. Dès le départ du projet, l'objectif du cabinet EMBT était la redécouverte des valeurs des espaces intérieurs du bâtiment néo-classique préexistant, spécialement la salle médiévale, rénovée auparavant en diverses occasions. D'autre part, les architectes souhaitaient revenir à l'idée d'un édifice municipal regroupant les diverses maisons de la ville, mêlant styles et matériaux distincts afin de refléter la diversité architecturale de la cité hollandaise. Afin d'accomplir cette intention, les travaux ont vu le recyclage de matériaux comme les briques, les chambranles et les linteaux de pierre provenant de la démolition de certaines parties de l'ancienne construction. Notons aussi que du fait de la complexité fonctionnelle, les activités ont été redistribuées afin que le rez-de-chaussée se convertisse en un entrelacement d'espaces publics, un tissu urbain couvert, et que le second niveau héberge la représentation politique.

Quest'incarico consisteva nell'ampliare la sede del comune di Utrecht, che era divenuta insufficiente ed era carente dei progressi tecnologici necessari in un organismo ufficiale. Fin dalla prima fase di progetto, l'obiettivo dello studio EMBT è stato quello di riscoprire il valore degli spazi interni dell'edificio neoclassico preesistente, specialmente quello della sala medievale, già restaurata in varie occasioni. D'altra parte gli architetti desideravano tornare all'idea di un edificio municipale come raggruppamento delle diverse case della città, che riunisse stili e materiali diversi come riflesso della diversità costruttiva della località olandese. Per mettere in pratica quest'intenzione, durante le opere furono riciclati materiali come mattoni, stipiti e architravi di pietra provenienti dalla demolizione di alcune parti del vecchio edificio. In seguito alla complessità funzionale, furono inoltre distribuite le attività in modo che il piano terra si è trasformato in un intreccio di spazi pubblici simile ad un tessuto urbano coperto, mentre il secondo piano ospita l'autorità politica.

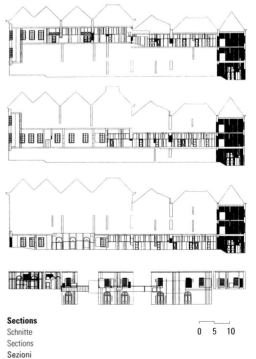

**Sections**
Schnitte
Sections
Sezioni

0  5  10

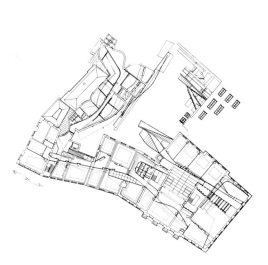

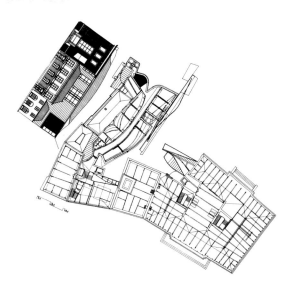

**Second floor and sections**
Zweites Obergeschoss und Schnitte
Deuxième étage et sections
Piano secondo e sezioni

**Structure plan and elevations**
Tragwerksplan und Aufrisse
Dessin de structure et élevations
Pianta della estruttura e prospetti

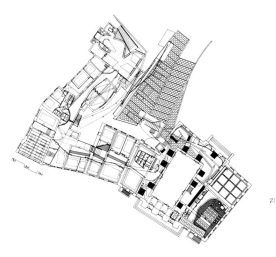

**Ground floor**
Erdgeschoss
Rez-de-chaussée
Piano terra

**First floor and elevations**
Erstes Obergeschoss und Aufrisse
Premier étage et élevations
Piano primo e prospetti

0   5   10

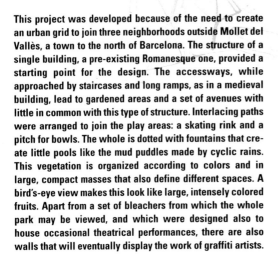

# Parc dels Colors

Location: Avinguda Caldes de Montbui 11-15, Mollet, Spain
Date of construction: 1992–2001
Photographer: Duccio Malagamba

This project was developed because of the need to create an urban grid to join three neighborhoods outside Mollet del Vallès, a town to the north of Barcelona. The structure of a single building, a pre-existing Romanesque one, provided a starting point for the design. The accessways, while approached by staircases and long ramps, as in a medieval building, lead to gardened areas and a set of avenues with little in common with this type of structure. Interlacing paths were arranged to join the play areas: a skating rink and a pitch for bowls. The whole is dotted with fountains that create little pools like the mud puddles made by cyclic rains. This vegetation is organized according to colors and in large, compact masses that also define different spaces. A bird's-eye view makes this look like large, intensely colored fruits. Apart from a set of bleachers from which the whole park may be viewed, and which were designed also to house occasional theatrical performances, there are also walls that will eventually display the work of graffiti artists.

Im Rahmen dieses Auftrags sollten drei Außenbezirke der Stadt Mollet del Vallès, nördlich von Barcelona, miteinander verbunden werden. Die Architekten gingen bei ihrer Planung von einem alten romanischen Gebäude aus. Doch obwohl der Zugang zum Gelände wie bei einem mittelalterlichen Bauwerk über Freitreppen und lange Rampen erfolgt, hat die Gestaltung der Grünflächen und die Entwicklung des Wegenetzes nicht mehr viel damit gemein. Die Wege sind so angelegt, dass sie die Spielplätze, d.h. die Rollschuhpiste und die Boule-Bahnen miteinander verbinden. Über das gesamte Gelände verteilt finden sich Fontänen, die in bestimmten Abständen Wasser sprühen und Pfützen entstehen lassen, ganz so wie bei zyklischen Regenfällen. Die Bepflanzung wurde nach der Farbgebung ausgewählt. Die dichten Vegetationsinseln trennen verschiedene Zonen des Parks voneinander. Von oben betrachtet wirken sie wie große Früchte in leuchtenden Farben. Weitere Gestaltungselemente sind die Tribüne, von der man die Gesamtanlage überblicken kann und vor der gelegentlich auch Theateraufführungen stattfinden, und lange Mauern, die dazu auffordern, mit Graffitis verziert zu werden.

La commande vient de la nécessité de créer un tissu urbain unissant trois quartiers de la périphérie de Mollet del Vallès, une localité située au nord de Barcelone. Au départ, le concept s'inspire de la structure d'un bâtiment roman existant. Bien que les accès s'offrent par des escaliers et larges rampes, comme dans un édifice médiéval, la disposition des espaces verts et des parcours a peu un commun avec ce type de construction. Un entrelacement de chemins a été disposé, uni par des zones de jeux, une piste de patinage et des pistes de pétanques. L'ensemble est, de plus, parsemé de fontaines intermittentes créant des flaques comme un pluie cyclique. La végétation a été organisée par couleurs, en grandes masses compactes définissant également différents espaces. Observées depuis les airs, elles ressemblent à de gigantesques fruits aux couleurs intenses. Hormis quelque gradins permettant de contempler tout le parc, pensés également pour accueillir des représentations théâtrales de temps à autre, ont été érigés des murs destinés à se convertir en un cadre idéal pour les graffitis.

L'incarico è nato dalla necessità di creare un tessuto urbano che unisse tre quartieri della periferia di Mollet del Vallès, una località situata a nord di Barcellona. Inizialmente il progetto ha tratto ispirazione dalla struttura di un edificio romanico esistente. Anche se gli ingressi avvengono attraverso delle scalinate e delle lunghe rampe, come in un edificio medievale, la disposizione delle zone verdi e dei percorsi non ha niente a che fare con questo tipo di costruzioni. Si è organizzato un tracciato di sentieri che unisce le zone gioco, una pista di pattinaggio e le aree per giocare a bocce; inoltre l'area è stata punteggiata di fontane intermittenti che creano pozzanghere come quelle della pioggia ciclica. La vegetazione è stata organizzata per colori, in grandi masse compatte che definiscono anche i diversi spazi. Viste dall'alto, sembrano grandi frutti di colore intenso. Oltre a una gradinata dalla quale si riesce a vedere tutto il parco, pensata anche per ospitare funzioni teatrali sporadiche, sono stati costruiti dei muri destinati a trasformarsi nella cornice ideale per dei graffiti.

**Plan**
Grundriss
Niveau
Pianta

0  5  10

Llull
Diagonal Mar
Mall
Avinguda Diagonal
Diagonal Mar
Park
Selva de Mar
Josep Pla
Rambla Prim
Passeig de Garcia Faria

# Diagonal Mar Park

Location: Selva de Mar/Llull/Josep Pla, Barcelona, Spain
Date of construction: 1997–2002
Photographer: Duccio Malagamba

For the construction of the installations of the 2004 Forum of Cultures, Barcelona City Council recovered a series of partially abandoned industrial lots near the sea. The urban reordering carried out on these configures a new neighborhood on the shores of the Mediterranean where a variety of activities are available. To connect Avinguda Diagonal, which crosses the whole city, with the beach a large park was created. EMBT organized the site via a road system that extends in different directions on a tree-like pattern. The main avenue directly connects the Avinguda Diagonal with the sea, passing over a pedestrian bridge that goes over the Ronda Litoral, a ring-road around the city. A series of spaces comes off the intersection of the roads and the points where they join the park. Here, skating rinks were installed, and games fields flanked by bicycle lanes. The water itself is of course present in almost every part of the park, whether in the guise of small ponds or as a very large lake that accompanies the main avenue along nearly all its length.

Für die Ausrichtung des Forums der Kulturen 2004 hat die Stadtverwaltung von Barcelona ein ehemaliges Industriegebiet in Meeresnähe ausgewählt. Im Rahmen der städtebaulichen Neuordnung dieses Bereichs entsteht am Mittelmeer ein neues Stadtviertel mit vielfältigen Nutzungsmöglichkeiten. Um die Avinguda Diagonal – eine breite Allee, die die gesamte Stadt durchquert – mit dem Strand zu verbinden, wurde ein großer Park geplant. EMBT entschied sich für ein Wegenetz, das sich wie das Astwerk eines Baumes in alle Richtungen verzweigt. Der Hauptweg führt von der Diagonal direkt ans Meer, wobei man unterwegs den Stadtautobahnring über eine Fußgängerbrücke überquert. An den Kreuzungspunkten der Wege und am Rand des Parks sind Rollschuhbahnen, Spielflächen und Fahrradwege geplant. Ein wichtiges Gestaltungselement im Park ist das Wasser. Es ist überall präsent, sei es in Form kleiner Teiche oder als großer See, an dem der Hauptweg entlangführt.

Pour la construction des installations du Forum des Cultures 2004, la municipalité a récupéré des terrains industriels partiellement abandonnés et proches de la mer. La réorganisation urbanistique menée à bien prête forme à un nouveau quartier au bord de la Méditerranée, où coexistent une diversité d'usages. Afin d'unir l'avenue Diagonal, traversant toute la ville, avec la plage, le projet d'un grand parc a été décidé. EMBT a organisé le terrain selon un système de chemins qui s'étendent dans toutes les directions, ainsi les branches d'un arbre. L'allée principale connecte directement la Diagonal à la mer, passant par un pont piétonnier couvrant la rocade Litoral, une voie rapide ceinturant la cité. De l'intersection des chemins et des points de confluence avec les limites du parc naissent une série d'espaces accueillant des pistes de patins, des parterres de jeu et des voies cyclables. L'eau est présente pratiquement à chaque instant, soit sous la forme de petits étangs ou celle d'un grand lac accompagnant la promenade principale sur tout son parcours.

Per la costruzione degli impianti del Foro delle Culture 2004, il comune di Barcellona ha recuperato dei terreni industriali parzialmente abbandonati vicino al mare. Il riassetto urbanistico portato a termine organizza un nuovo quartiere sulle rive del Mediterraneo dove convivono una gran varietà di usi. Per unire il viale Diagonal, che attraversa tutta la città, alla spiaggia, è stato deciso di progettare un grande parco. EMBT ha organizzato il terreno mediante un sistema di percorsi che si estendono in tutte le direzioni, come i rami di un albero. Il percorso principale collega direttamente la Diagonal con il mare, passando attraverso un ponte pedonale che copre la circonvallazione del Litoral, una strada rapida che circonda la città. All'intersezione dei sentieri ed ai limiti del parco nascono una serie di spazi dove sono state situate piste di pattinaggio, parterre di gioco e percorsi ciclistici. L'acqua è presente in quasi tutta la superficie del parco, sia in forma di piccoli stagni o nel grande lago che accompagna, lungo quasi tutto il suo percorso, il viale principale.

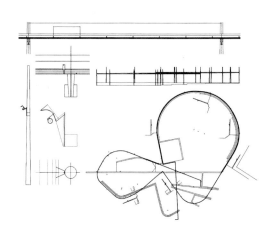

**Details**
Details
Détails
Dettagli

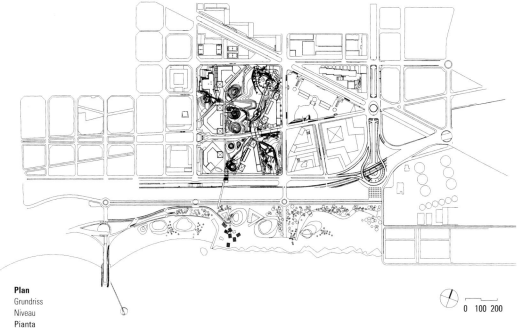

**Plan**
Grundriss
Niveau
Pianta

0  100 200

# Campus of the University of Vigo

Location: Rúa Oporto 1, Vigo, Spain
Date of construction: 1999–2003
Photographers: Alex Gaultier, Lourdes Jansana

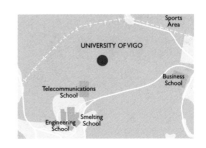

The project analyzed the configuration of the entrance to the campus of the University of Vigo, in Galice, the transformation of the sports area, urbanization of the new commercial zone, and the introduction of a parking complex. The campus has undergone a change in the wake of the EMBT studio's work, a project that transformed the place into a unified constructed landscape. One of the accessways to this landscape is by way of the sports area, and this includes a wide-sweeping reforestation of the terrain as well as the installation of a series of ponds. Thus, the visitor penetrates the complex by way of a lush woodland, and the students can exercise among the trees. The commercial area gives the place a mall and residence halls in buildings that conflate with the topography: this is partially accomplished by penetrating the open plaza with a metallic mesh canopy held up by columns and roofed in tropical wood. The opaque façades of the different buildings are covered in concrete faced in granite. The roofs, also of concrete, serve as home to the restaurant, accessed by the central staircase of the assembly.

Das Projekt umfasst den Eingangsbereich zum Campus der Universität Vigo in Galicien, die Umgestaltung der Sportanlagen, die Errichtung von Ladenlokalen und Wohnungen und den Bau eines Parkplatzes. Die vom Büro EMBT geplanten Maßnahmen lassen das Universitätsgelände zu einer zusammenhängenden Baulandschaft werden. Einer der Zugänge zum Campus liegt bei den Sportanlagen. Dort wurde aufgeforstet und es wurden einige kleine Teiche angelegt. Nun gelangt man durch einen dichten Wald auf das Gelände und die Studenten können zwischen den Bäumen Sport treiben. Das Einkaufszentrum mit den Wohnungen passt sich den topografischen Gegebenheiten an. Der Komplex schiebt sich mit einem von Pfeilern getragenen und mit tropischem Holz gedeckten Vordach aus Metall auf den Platz vor. Bei den fensterlosen Fassaden wurde die Betonstruktur mit Granit verkleidet. Über dem Betondach befindet sich ein Restaurant, das über die zentrale Treppenanlage zu erreichen ist.

Le projet a étudié la configuration de l'entrée du campus de l'Université de Vigo, en Galice, la transformation de la zone sportive, l'urbanisation du nouveau secteur commercial et la construction d'un parc de stationnement. Le campus a connu un changement après l'intervention du cabinet EMBT, transformant le lieu en un paysage construit unitaire. Un des entrées à l'enceinte s'effectue entre les pistes de sports. La décision a donc été prise de reboiser amplement le terrain et de projeter une série de petits lacs. Ainsi, le visiteur pénètre dans le complexe sous les frondaisons et les étudiants peuvent s'exercer entre les arbres. La zone commerciale dote le complexe de boutiques et de logements dans des volumes liés à la topographie et envahissant l'espace de la place avec une marquise métallique soutenues par des piliers et couverte de bois d'elondo. Les façades opaques des divers volumes sont en béton revêtu de granit et sur la toiture, également en béton, a été situé le restaurant, accessible par l'escalier central de l'ensemble.

Il progetto ha studiato la disposizione dell'entrata del campus dell'Università di Vigo, a Galicia, la trasformazione della zona sportiva, l'urbanizzazione della nuova zona commerciale e la costruzione di un parcheggio. Il campus, dopo l'intervento dello studio EMBT, ha subito un cambiamento che ha trasformato il luogo in un paesaggio costruito unitario. Uno degli accessi al recinto avviene passando tra le piste sportive, per cui è stato deciso di rimboscare ampiamente il terreno e di progettare una serie di piccoli laghi. In questo modo il visitatore entra nel complesso attraverso un rigoglioso bosco e gli studenti possono fare esercizio tra gli alberi. La zona commerciale dota il complesso di negozi ed alloggi adattati alla topografia del terreno, che invadono lo spazio della piazza con una tettoia metallica sostenuta da pilastri e coperta di legno tropicale. Le facciate opache dei diversi volumi sono di cemento rivestito di granito e sulla copertura, anch'essa in cemento, è stato collocato il ristorante, al quale si accede attraverso la scala centrale del complesso.

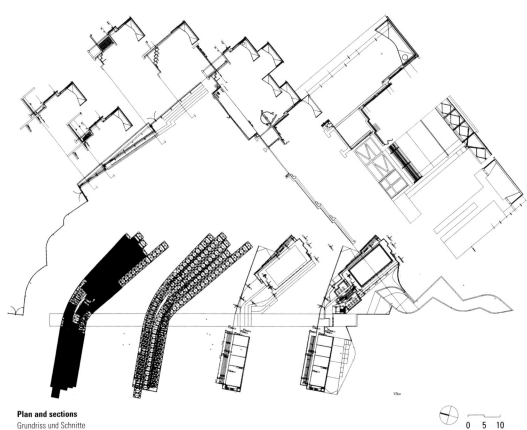

**Plan and sections**
Grundriss und Schnitte
Niveau et sections
Pianta e sezioni

0   5   10

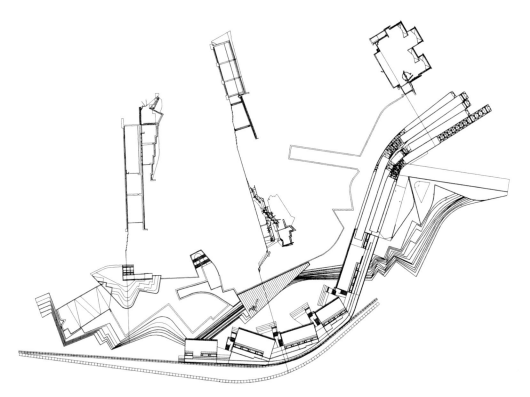

**Roof plan and sections**
Grundriss der Dächer und Schnitte
Niveau supérieur et sections
Pianta delle coperture e sezioni

# Scottish Parliament

Location: Holyrood Road, Edinburgh, Scotland, UK
Date of construction: 1998–2003
Photographers: Lourdes Jansana, EMBT Arquitectes

In 1998, EMBT won, from among thirty participants, the bid to raise the new Edinburgh Parliament building. The proposal generated great enthusiasm due to its organic capacity to combine extant elements with new technologies through the contemporary and unique language of the Barcelona studio. The project's development centered on reflecting the characteristics of the country and its inhabitants via a new way of building that was directly linked to the land itself. This close tie to the site and its setting will, when the adjacent distillery is demolished, enable the generation of multiple perspective lines on the city. Intentionally, a contrast is sought, a conceptual distance, between the new edification and Holyrood Palace, the twelfth-century royal residence repeatedly rehabilitated at different times. Unlike the palace, which dominates the landscape, the new Scottish Parliament drops literally into the hillside terrain, the lowest part of the so-called King Arthur's Seat, and appears to sprout from the living stone.

Im Jahre 1998 setzte sich das Büro EMBT in der Ausschreibung zur Errichtung des neuen schottischen Parlaments in Edinburg gegen 30 Mitbewerber durch. Der Entwurf besticht durch die Fähigkeit der Architekten aus Barcelona, alte Elemente in einzigartiger zeitgenössischer Formensprache organisch mit neuer Technik zu verbinden. Der Entwurf soll die Eigenarten des Landes und seiner Bewohner widerspiegeln und wirkt daher sehr erdverbunden. Das Gebäude steht in enger Beziehung zur Landschaft, außerdem werden zahlreiche Sichtachsen zum Stadtkern freigelegt. Der Neubau gibt sich in der Auffassung distanziert und steht in bewusstem Kontrast zum königlichen Schloss Holyrood, das im 12. Jahrhundert errichtet und immer wieder umgestaltet wurde. Anders als das Schloss, das sich über der Landschaft erhebt, fügt sich das schottische Parlament in die Erde ein, scheint aus dem Fels zu entspringen, schmiegt sich an den Hang des Hügels, der als Thron König Artus bekannt ist.

En 1998, le cabinet d'EMBT a remporté, parmi trente participants, le concours de construction du nouveau bâtiment du Parlement d'Édimbourg. La proposition a enthousiasmé par sa capacité organique à combiner des éléments anciens avec de nouvelles technologies grâce au langage actuel et singulier du cabinet barcelonais. Le développement du projet s'est centré sur la réflexion des caractéristiques du pays et de ses habitants grâce à un édifice ancré dans la terre. Cette relation si étroite avec le terrain et son cadre permettrait de générer de multiples axes de vue vers le centre de la ville. Un contraste, une distance conceptuelle ont été recherchées entre la nouvelle construction et le palais Holyrood, la résidence royale construite au XIIème siècle et réhabilitée à diverses reprises par la suite. À la différence du palais, se détachant dans le paysage, le nouveau parlement écossais est littéralement serti dans le lieu, sur le versant de la colline connue sous le nom de Trône du roi Arthur, jaillissant presque de la roche.

Nel 1998, lo studio EMBT ha vinto, fra trenta partecipanti, il concorso per erigere il nuovo edificio del Parlamento di Edimburgo. La proposta ha entusiasmato per la capacità organica di combinare elementi antichi a nuove tecnologie, attraverso il linguaggio attuale ed originale dello studio di Barcellona. L'elaborazione del progetto si è centrata nel riflettere le caratteristiche del paese e dei suoi abitanti mediante una costruzione radicata alla terra. Questa relazione così stretta col terreno ed il suo ambiente circostante permetterà di generare molteplici assi visuali diretti al centro della città. Intenzionalmente è stato ricercato un contrasto, una distanza concettuale, tra la nuova costruzione ed il palazzo Holyrood, la residenza reale costruita nel XII° secolo e restaurata in diverse occasioni in epoche successive. A differenza del palazzo, che spicca sul paesaggio, il nuovo Parlamento scozzese è stato inserito letteralmente nel terreno, nelle pendici della collina conosciuta col nome di Trono del re Arturo, quasi come se nascesse dalla roccia.

**Elevation**
Aufriss
Élévation
Prospetto

**Longitudinal section**
Längsschnitt
Section longitudinale
Sezione longitudinale

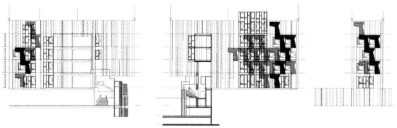

**Elevations**
Aufrisse
Élévations
Prospetti

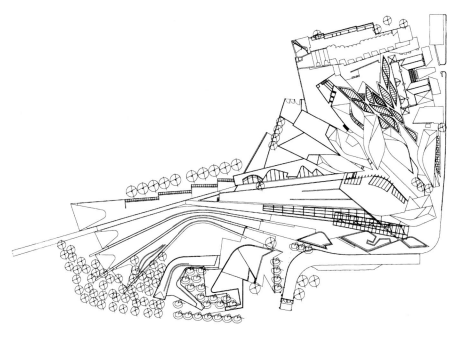

**Plan**
Grundriss
Niveau
Pianta

0  5  10

# Restoration of Santa Caterina Market

Location: Avinguda Francesc Cambó, Barcelona, Spain
Date of construction: 1997–2004
Photographers: Manel Quadrada, EMBT Arquitectes

**In 1997, a competition was opened to restore the city market, Santa Caterina, in the old quarter of Barcelona, near the cathedral. The EMBT studio won the bid with a proposal that aimed at incorporating the very complexity of the setting itself to generate a commercial mall project complemented by a residential zone and public spaces that made all neighborhood activities a part of the overall renewal. From the word go the idea of demolishing the extant structures was rejected. A new image was to be set in operation while the market remained part of the history of the place. This choice superimposes new architecture on old, mixes them, and comes up with a conglomerate, a hybrid that accentuates usefulness and contemporaneity. It fronts the perception of the development of the building. The interior distribution of the market has been reorganized; there are fewer stands but the access and service systems are rationalized; the surface area of public spaces gains ground and communicates with the Avingunda Francesc Cambó, an important artery in the neighborhood, and with the dense network of narrow streets.**

En 1997 un concours a été ouvert pour réhabiliter le marché municipal de Santa Caterina, situé dans le centre ancien de Barcelone, près de la cathédrale. Le cabinet EMBT a emporté la commande avec une proposition suggérant de profiter de l'environnement pour générer un projet où l'usage commercial serait complété par le résidentiel et les espaces publics, entrelaçant toutes les activités du quartier. Depuis le départ, la possibilité de démolir l'ensemble existant a été repoussée. Il s'agissait d'intégrer la nouvelle image dans l'histoire du lieu. Ainsi, les nouvelles constructions se superposent à l'existant, se mêlant et s'érigeant en un conglomérat, un hybride utile et contemporain permettant de percevoir la trajectoire de l'édifice. La distribution intérieure du marché a été réorganisée. Ont été prévus moins d'emplacements mais les systèmes d'accès et de service ont été rationalisés. De plus, la superficie d'espace public a été maximisée, afin de faire communiquer l'avenue Francesc Cambó, une artère importante du quartier, avec l'intérieur du district, aux rues plus étroites et au maillage plus dense.

Im Jahre 1997 wurde ein Wettbewerb für den Umbau der städtischen Markthalle Santa Caterina in Barcelona ausgeschrieben, die nahe der Kathedrale in der Altstadt liegt. Das Büro EMBT gewann den Wettbewerb mit einem Vorschlag, der die Komplexität des umgebenden Stadtraums zum Anlass für ein Projekt nahm, das die kommerzielle Nutzung mit Wohnungen und öffentlichen Einrichtungen verbindet, um alle Aktivitäten des Viertels an dieser Stelle zu bündeln. Die Mauern der Markthalle sollten auf jeden Fall erhalten bleiben. Ziel war es, das neu geschaffene äußere Erscheinungsbild in die Geschichte des Ortes zu integrieren. Die neuen Bauten überlagern daher die alten, vermischen sich mit ihnen und bilden ein Konglomerat, das in seiner hybriden Ausformung, die zugleich nützlich und zeitgemäß ist, die historische Entwicklung des Gebäudes nachvollziehbar werden lässt. Die innere Aufteilung der Markthalle wurde neu geordnet: Es sind weniger Stände vorgesehen und die Zugänge und Dienstleistungsbereiche werden übersichtlicher gestaltet. Bei den Außenanlagen ist eine Erweiterung des öffentlichen Bereichs vorgesehen, um die Avingunda Francesc Cambó, eine wichtige Erschließungsstraße, an das Geflecht der schmalen Gassen des Viertels anzubinden.

Nel 1997 è stato bandito un concorso per ristrutturare il mercato comunale di Santa Caterina, situato nel centro storico di Barcellona, vicino al duomo. Lo studio EMBT ha vinto il concorso con una proposta che suggeriva di utilizzare la complessità dell'intorno urbano per generare un progetto dove l'uso commerciale fosse integrato da quello residenziale e da spazi pubblici che collegassero tutte le attività del quartiere. Fin dal principio è stata scartata la possibilità di demolire il complesso esistente. Si trattava di far sì che la nuova immagine continuasse a formar parte della storia del luogo. In questo modo le nuove costruzioni si sovrappongono a quelle esistenti, si mescolano e si innalzano come un agglomerato, un ibrido utile e contemporaneo che permette di percepire la traiettoria dell'edificio. La distribuzione interna del mercato è stata riorganizzata; sono state previste meno bancarelle ma sono stati razionalizzati i sistemi d'accesso e di servizio, ed è stata inoltre garantita una maggior superficie di spazio pubblico, che comunicherà il corso Francesc Cambó, un'arteria importante del quartiere, con l'interno della circoscrizione, fatto di strade molto più strette e con una tessuto più denso.

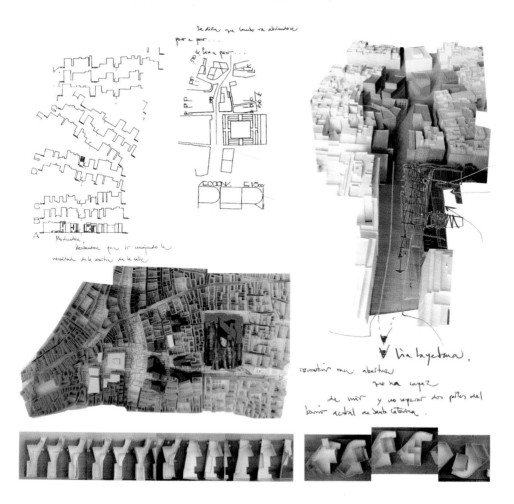

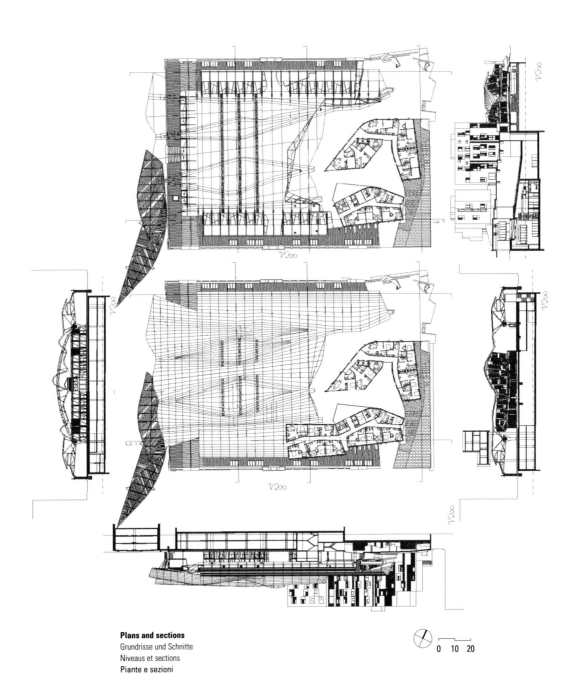

**Plans and sections**
Grundrisse und Schnitte
Niveaus et sections
Piante e sezioni

0 10 20

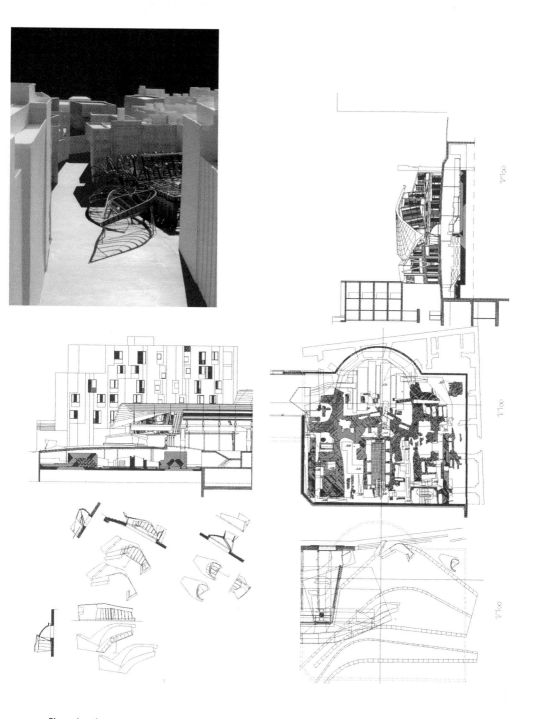

**Plan and sections**
Grundriss und Schnitte
Niveau et sections
Pianta e sezioni

# Istituto Universitario di Architettura di Venezia

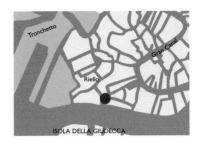

Location: Venice, Italy
Date of competition: 1998
Photographer: Lourdes Jansana

The new headquarters of the Istituto Universitario di Architettura di Venezia (IUAV) occupies a former industrial warehouse that was used as a refrigerated storage chamber. It is located in the San Basilio neighborhood, a manufacturing zone which the municipal and port authorities want to reinsert in the city's urban grid. The program for this project includes classrooms, a conference hall with a capacity for 500 people plus exhibition rooms. But also foreseen is the availability of service and communication spaces which should be flexible. These last features must in fact provide the framework for multi-use activities. The proposal is attentive and respectful of the pre-existing architecture, certainly. The planning includes a large staircase which serves as a leisure and meeting zone for students. From the vestibule accessed by the stairway juts a ramp to the catwalk bridge joining the present headquarters of the institute. Elevators and stairs lead to the classrooms and also to terraces that provide panoramas of the city. At street level, a bar-restaurant, bookstore, and auditorium are arranged around an indoor patio.

Der neue Sitz des Istituto Universitario di Architettura di Venezia (IUAV) wurde in einer ehemaligen Lagerhalle eingerichtet, die als Kühlhaus gedient hatte. Das Gebäude liegt im Viertel San Basilio, einem Industriegebiet, das Stadt- und Hafenverwaltung wieder an die Stadt anbinden wollen. Das Projekt sieht Unterrichtsräume, einen Konferenzsaal für 500 Zuhörer und Ausstellungsflächen vor. Außerdem ist eine große Flexibilität bei der Raumgestaltung des öffentlichen Bereichs vorgesehen, in dem die verschiedensten Veranstaltungen stattfinden können. Die Architekten gehen mit der vorhandenen Bausubstanz sehr behutsam um und schlagen eine breite Freitreppe vor, die zugleich als Versammlungsort und Ruhezone für die Studenten dient. Aus der Vorhalle, zu der man über diese Treppe gelangt, führt eine Rampe zu einer Brücke, die das neue Gebäude mit dem ehemaligen Sitz des Instituts verbindet. Über Fahrstühle und Treppen sind die Klassenräume zu erreichen und ebenso die Terrassen, von denen aus man einen Ausblick auf die Stadt hat. Zu ebener Erde sind um einen Innenhof ein Café-Restaurant, eine Buchhandlung und der große Hörsaal angeordnet.

Le nouveau siège de l'Istituto Universitario di Architettura di Venezia (IUAV) occupe un ancien entrepôt industriel servant de chambre frigorifique et situé dans le quartier de San Basilio, une zone de manufacture que les autorités municipales et portuaires veulent insérer à nouveau dans le tissu urbain de la cité. Le programme du projet inclut des salles de cours, une salle de conférence pour 500 personnes et des aires d'exposition. Mais il est aussi prévu de lui conférer une grande flexibilité pour les espaces de services et de communication, devant constituer le cadre d'activités multiples. La proposition, attentive et respectueuse avec la construction existante, dispose un grand escalier devant servir de lieu de réunion et de repos pour les étudiants. Depuis le hall auquel mènent les marches naît une rampe qui accède au pont établissant la liaison avec le siège actuel de l'institution. Ascenseurs et escaliers conduisent aux salles de cours et aux terrasses offrant des vues sur la ville. Au niveau de la rue, un bar-restaurant, la bibliothèque et l'auditorium sont distribués autour d'un patio intérieur.

La nuova sede dell'Istituto Universitario di Architettura di Venezia (IUAV) occupa un antico magazzino, utilizzato come camera frigorifera, situato nel quartiere di San Basilio, una zona industriale che l'amministrazione comunale e quella portuaria vogliono reinserire nel tessuto urbano della città. Il programma di progetto include aule, una sala conferenze da 500 posti e varie superfici espositive. È previsto inoltre che gli spazi di servizio e di comunicazione, che devono costituire lo sfondo di numerose attività, dispongano di gran flessibilità. La proposta, attenta e rispettosa della costruzione esistente, propone una grande scalinata che servirà come luogo di riunione e riposo per gli studenti. Dall'ingresso al quale giungono le scale parte, a sua volta, una rampa che dà accesso al ponte che mette in comunicazione con l'attuale sede dell'istituto. Ascensori e scale conducono alle aule e a delle terrazze che offrono interessanti panoramiche della città. All'altezza della strada, disposti intorno ad un cortile interno, si trovano un bar-ristorante, la libreria e l'auditorium.

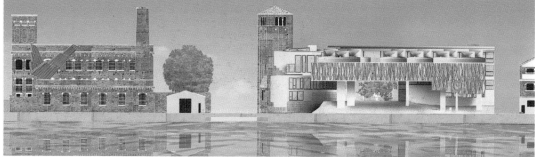

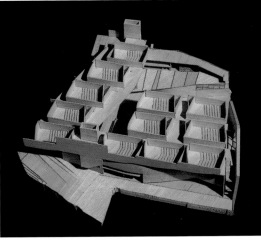

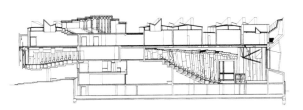

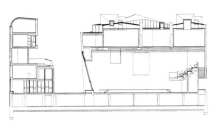

**Sections**
Schnitte
Sections
Sezioni

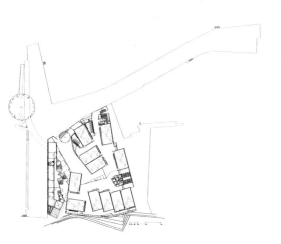

**Third floor**
Drittes Obergeschoss
Troième étage
Piano terzo

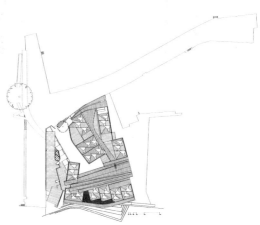

**Roof plan**
Grundriss der Dächer
Niveau supérieur
Pianta delle coperture

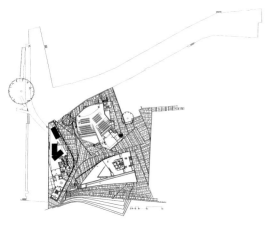

**Ground floor**
Erdgeschoss
Rez-de-chaussée
Piano terra

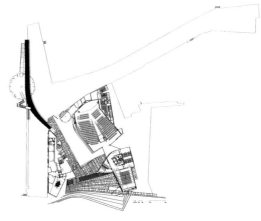

**Second floor**
Zweites Obergeschoss
Deuxième étage
Piano secondo

0 10 20

# Gas Natural Headquarters

Location: Avinguda Salvat Papasseit, Barcelona, Spain
Date of construction: 1999–2005
Photographers: EMBT Arquitectes

The company Gas Natural decided to abandon its main building in the historical center of Barcelona. The new headquarters is a tower of 22 stories which is 86 meters high. EMBT created this project for the company in the Barceloneta neighborhood, very close to the sea. The project involved raising a unique tower capable of enriching the city skyline and also respecting the small dimensions of the buildings that make up the district of Barceloneta, an area where fisher families' houses coexist with five-story apartment blocks. From the outset, the project was designed to be compatible with these two main premises. This meant planning for different volumes with different sizes and characteristics that would still make up a definite unit. The work thus responds to different scales and enables the establishment of a physical dialogue with the nearby buildings. But it also rises up as a new city landmark. Finally, special attention was given to the new exterior spaces.

Als das Unternehmen Gas Natural beschloss, seinen Stammsitz in der historischen Altstadt aufzugeben und in einen Neubau am Meer im Viertel Barceloneta umzuziehen, entwarf das Büro EMBT für den Konzern ein 86 Meter hohes, 22-stöckiges Bürohaus. Eine besondere Herausforderung des Projekts bestand darin, die Silhouette der Stadt um einen markanten Turm zu bereichern und zugleich die Maßstäbe eines Viertels zu respektieren, in dem es neben alten Fischerhäusern Wohnblocks mit einer Höhe von höchstens fünf Stockwerken gibt. Von Anfang an sollte das Projekt diesen beiden Anforderungen gerecht werden, weshalb sich die Architekten für einen Gebäudekomplex entschieden, der aus Baukörpern unterschiedlicher Form und Größe besteht. So ist gewährleistet, dass der Neubau die Proportionen der benachbarten Bebauung im Dialog aufnehmen und sich doch zugleich als weithin sichtbares Signal über die Stadt erheben kann. Besonderes Augenmerk galt den Außenanlagen.

La compagnie Gas Natural a décidé d'abandonner son siège du centre historique de Barcelone afin d'occuper la nouvelle tour de 22 étages pour 86 mètres de haut, projetée par EMBT pour l'entreprise dans le quartier de la Barceloneta, proche de la mer. Le défi portait sur l'érection d'une tour unique, à même d'enrichir la silhouette de la cité tout en respectant les dimensions réduites des immeubles formant le quartier, un lieu de coexistence d'anciennes maisons de pêcheurs et de blocs de cinq étages au plus. Dès le départ, le projet a été pensé pour être compatible avec ces deux présupposés. De ce fait ont vu le jour divers volumes aux dimensions et aux caractéristiques distinctes afin de conformer un ensemble unitaire. Ainsi, l'œuvre répond à diverses échelles et peut établir un dialogue physique avec les édifices proches tout en s'élevant comme un phare de la cité. Une attention spéciale a également été portée aux espaces extérieurs résultants.

La compagnia Gas Natural decise di abbandonare la sua sede nel centro storico di Barcellona per occupare il nuovo grattacielo di 22 piani e 86 metri d'altezza, che EMBT ha progettato per la ditta nel quartiere della Barceloneta, vicino al mare. La sfida era innalzare una torre singolare, capace di arricchire il profilo della città ed allo stesso tempo rispettare le ridotte dimensioni degli edifici che compongono la circoscrizione, dove convivono vecchie case di pescatori con condomini al massimo di cinque piani. Fin dal principio si è pensato in un progetto compatibile con queste due premesse, così che sono stati progettati vari volumi, di misure e caratteristiche diverse, che conformassero un insieme unitario. In questo modo l'opera risponde alle diverse scale e può stabilire un dialogo fisico con le costruzioni vicine, ma allo stesso tempo può costituire un caposaldo nella città. È stata prestata particolare attenzione anche agli spazi esterni di risulta.

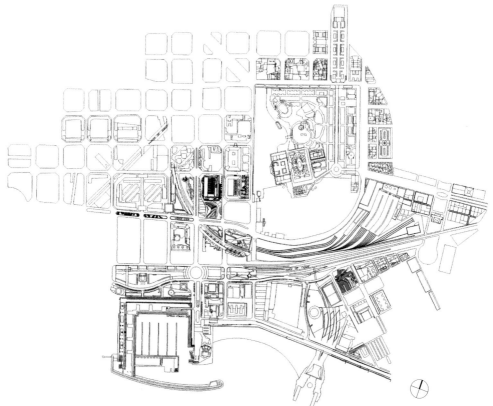

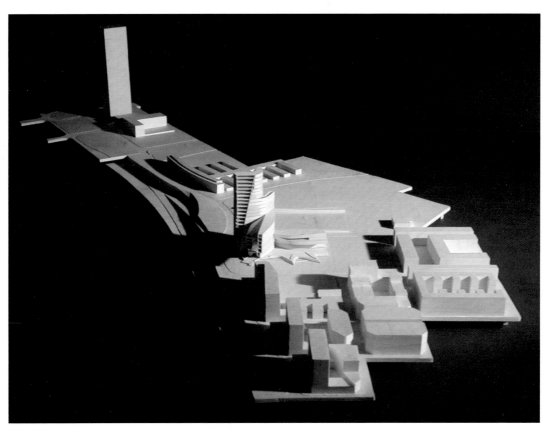

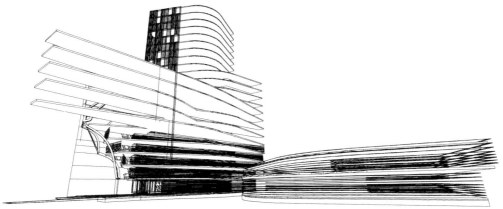

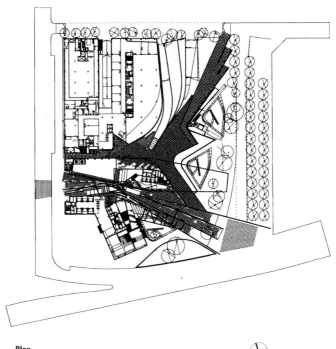

**Plan**
Grundriss
Niveau
Pianta

0  15  30

# Hafencity

Location: Hamburg, Germany
Date of construction: 2002
Photographer: Lourdes Jansana

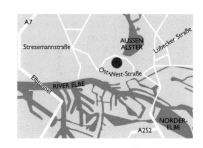

The society managing the development of the Port of Hamburg set up a competition to regenerate and urbanize the shores of the River Elbe in the town center. The proposal launched by the EMBT studio won with a project that stands out by its offer of a great diversity of spaces to allow Hamburg's inhabitants and visitors to take advantage of the nearby waterway. The intervention is organized on three levels: zero grade, at river level, is made up of gigantic platforms that access small craft and recreational boats. On the line of docks, 4.5 meters above sea-level, two rest areas were designed; and on the 7.5 meter (street) level, avenues were laid out, and gardened spaces with pergolas that accompany city visitors on their tours. A system of ramps, stairways, and catwalks connects the different levels. One of the project's most welcome protagonists is the vegetation: there are many different types and the addition will change the look of the port according to the season of the year, a note of color and contrasts for the northern city.

Die Gesellschaft, die für die Umstrukturierung des Hamburger Hafens verantwortlich war, schrieb einen Wettbewerb zur Neugestaltung des Elbufers im Stadtzentrum aus, bei dem das Büro EMBT mit seinem Vorschlag gewann. Das Projekt sieht eine Vielzahl unterschiedlicher Bereiche vor, in denen die Bewohner und Besucher der Hansestadt die Nähe des Wassers genießen können. Es sind drei Ebenen geplant: Die unterste, auf gleicher Höhe mit dem Wasser, besteht aus riesigen Plattformen, über die man zu Booten und Ausflugsschiffen gelangt. Auf der Höhe der Kais, also 4,5 Meter über dem Wasserspiegel, sind Ruhezonen vorgesehen und auf Straßenebene, d.h. bei etwa 7,5 Meter, sollen Spazierwege, Grünflächen und Laubengänge für Fußgänger entstehen. Über ein System von Rampen, Treppen und Stegen sind die drei Ebenen miteinander verbunden. Eine besondere Rolle spielt die Vegetation: Ausgewählte Pflanzenarten werden im Laufe der Jahreszeiten wechselnde Farbakzente im Hafen setzen.

La société gérant le développement du port de Hambourg a convoqué un concours afin de régénérer et d'urbaniser les berges de l'Elbe, au centre de la ville. La proposition du cabinet EMBT a remporté la soumission avec un projet offrant une grande diversité d'espaces afin que les habitants et visiteurs profitent de la proximité de l'eau. L'intervention s'organise selon trois niveaux : la cote zéro, au niveau de l'eau, est formée par de gigantesques plates-formes facilitant l'accès aux petits bateaux et aux embarcations de loisirs. Alignées avec les quais, 4,5 mètres au dessus du niveau de la mer, ont été conçues des aires de repos et, au niveau de la rue, à la cote 7,5 mètres, des allées, espaces paysagers et pergolas ont été tracés afin d'accompagner le visiteur le long de son parcours. Un système de rampes, d'escaliers et de passerelles connecte les niveaux distincts. La végétation est l'un des éléments principaux du projet, des variétés diverses modifiant l'aspect du port selon la saison de l'année et apportant couleurs et contrastes à cette cité du nord.

La società che gestisce lo sviluppo del porto di Amburgo ha bandito un concorso per riformare ed urbanizzare le rive del fiume Elba, nel centro della città. La proposta dello studio EMBT ha vinto il bando con un progetto che offre una gran diversità di spazi perché i abitanti e visitatori godano della vicinanza con l'acqua. L'intervento è sviluppato su tre livelli: la quota zero, all'altezza dell'acqua, è costituita da alcune piattaforme giganti che permettono l'accesso a piccole barche ed alle imbarcazioni da diporto. All'altezza dei moli, 4,5 metri sul livello del mare, è stata progettata la zona di sosta; ed all'altezza della strada, a quota 7,5 metri, sono stati tracciati percorsi, spazi verdi e pergolati che accompagnano il visitatore lungo la passeggiata. Un sistema di rampe, scale e passerelle collega i diversi livelli. Uno degli elementi protagonisti del progetto è la vegetazione, composta da diverse varietà che cambieranno l'aspetto del porto secondo la stagione dell'anno, ed apporteranno vivacità e contrasto in questa città nordica.

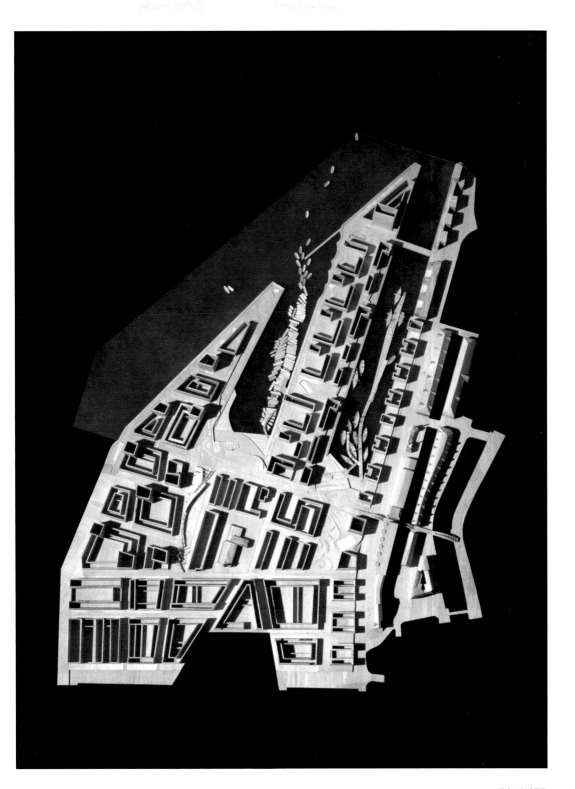

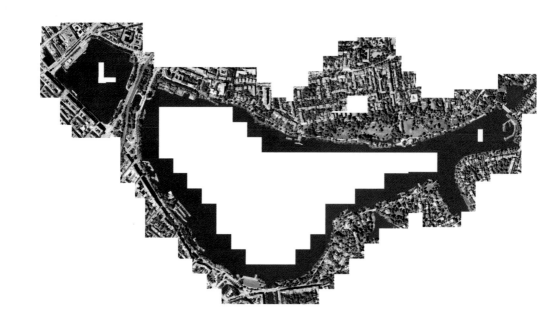

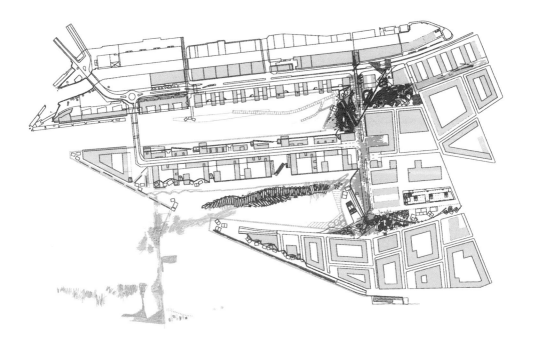

**Plan**
Grundriss
Niveau
Pianta

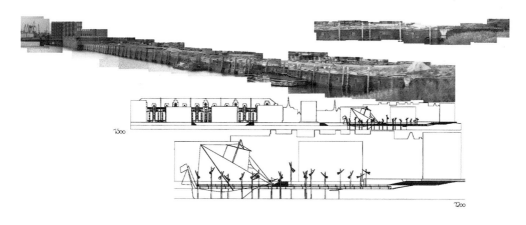

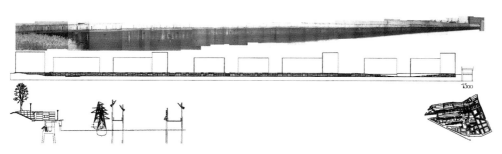

**Sections**
Schnitte
Sections
Sezioni

**Detail**
Detail
Détail
Dettaglio

# Credits

Key persons in this office, under every point of view, are: Elena Rocchi, Joan Callís, Karl Unglaub, Daniel Rosselló...

### House in Carrer Mercaders
Principals in charge: E.M. + B.T.
Landscape design: E.M. + B.T., Jardineria Moix
Structural engineer: R. Brufau
Quantity surveyor: Jordi Altes
Constructor: Tierra y Mar SA

### House in La Clota
Principals in charge: E.M. + B.T., Josep Ustrell
EMBT collaborators: N. Lund Overgaard, S. Le Draoullec, V. Sarnthein, N.M. Larsen, Prisca, R. Jiménez, R. Flores, K. Mayfield, L. Freed (model workshop)
Structural engineers: Manuel Barreras, Josep Ustrell, Jordi Bernuz
Constructor: ARPE SL
Brickwork, electrical, lighting, and finishes: ARPE SL
Carpentry, glazing, paintwork: Josep Figuera
Steelwork, iron mongery: Esteve Miret, ESMART

### School of Music
Principals in charge: E.M. + B.T., Karl Unglaub
EMBT collaborators:
Basic and execution project: Karl Unglaub, Torsten Skoetz, Nuno Jacinto, T. Kappel, O. Schmidt, E. Frances, S. Panis, A. Birr, F. Brancatelli, W. Fok, S. Techen, V. Thake, L. Gestin, M. Hamann, L. Giovanozzi, A.M. Henao, T. Stauss, M. Lechelt, M. Coing Maillet, A.G. Caspado, S. Belli, S. Hay (model wokshop)
Competition: Karl Unglaub, Elena Rocchi, Fabián Asunción (head of model workshop), L. Hainz, S. Gosmann, C.A. Ruiz, M. Eichorn
Execution Associate office: NPS + PARTNER, ARCHITEKTEN BDA, Hamburg
General contractor: GB Immobilien Gmbh., Hamburg; General Planners: ECE
Project management: Gmbh. & Co. KG, Hamburg, F.W. Frenzel
General Construction: Strabag Hoch-und Ingenieurbau AG, Berlin; Static Engineer: Windels, Timm, Morgen, Hamburg
Acoustic Engineer: Wolfgang Jensen, Hamburg; Electronic Engineer: Ingenieurbüro HSP, Hamburg
Landscape Architects: Rüppel & Rüppel, Hamburg; Façade Engineer: IFFT, Institut für Fassadentechnik

### Utrecht Town Hall
Principals in charge: E.M. + B.T., Marc de Rooij
EMBT project collaborators:
Basic and execution project: C. Chara, C. Hitz, S. Becaus, F. McArdle, F. Tata, Fabián Asunción (head of model workshop), A. M. Henao, C. Egger, S. Hay, L. Giovannozzi, J. Gassman, A. Latour, M. Coing Mailler, R. Alessandroni, A. Catania (model workshop)
Competition: Ricardo Flores, Elena Rocchi, G. Zambrana, M. Forteza Parera, N.-M. Larsen, N. Lund Overgaard, A. Floros, M. Carrión, A. Galmar (project collaborators), Fabián Asunción (head of model workshop), M. Carrera, L. Bonforte, G. La Cognata, M. Ortlieb, L. Tonella, S. Eckert, U. Grölz, J. Koettgen, C. Himmler (model workshop)
Associate Architect collaborators: De ArchitectenGroep, Bjarne Mastenbroek, Dick van Gameren
Project manager: B. Joziasse, DHV
Architect collaborator: J. Slot, INBO Adviseurs
Construction engineers: F. Schreuders, Pieters Bouwtechniek Utrecht BV, S. Fisher, Ove Arup & Partners
Installation engineers: R. Philippi, Theo Perotti, Cumae BV; Lighting engineers: HYP Oostenbrugge, D&H Group
Interior: AGM Smeulders, Smeulders Interieur werken BV

## Parcs dels Colors

**Architects in charge:** E.M. + B.T.,Lluis Cantallops
**EMBT project collaborators:**
**Basic and execution project:** Joan Callís, J. Miàs, R. Flores, J. Cargol, J. Artigues, M.R. Greene, L. De Colle, N. Álvarez, V. Garriga, S. Maurer, G. Zambran, H. Poppinghaus, U. Viotto
**Preliminary Design:** Ricardo Flores, Josep Cargol, P. Wortham, M. Lluch, A. M. Henao Sanabria (model workshop)
**Project Management:** G3, Jordi Altés
**Services:** PGI, Josep Juliol and Josep Masachs
**Structures:** Ove Arup & Partners, Madrid (1th phase); Miguel Barreras, CEA (2nd and 3rd phase); J.C. Adell, Ricard Pi and Ricardo Serra
**Constructor:** Copcisa Laia Codina, ALM-4, Bonal

## Diagonal Mar Park

**Architects in charge:** B.T., Elena Rocchi, Lluís Cantallops
**EMBT project collaborators:**
**Execution project :** Fabián Asunción, Mònica Batalla, E. Cattaneo, R. Sforza, M. Fukuda, L. Valentini, M. Chizzola, C. Hofler, S. Geenen (project collaborators)
**1st phase:** M. Eichhorn, S. Eckert, C. Himmler, G. Mahnke, W.L. Hainz, J.M. Grebe, F. Tata, A. Floros, P. Comacchio, A. Catania, U. Stübner, A. Möller, H. Koizumi, D. Rosselló, M. Fukuda, K. Sato, A. Versuere, Fabián Asunción (head of model workshop), I. Zaragoza, A. Möller, I. Sambeth, L. Bonforte, T. Gottschalk, L. Tonella, J. Koettgen, T. Aus Der Beek, C. Bojsen-Möller, M. Carrera Vázquez, F. Jacques-Dias, S. Gosmann, P. Lauper, A. Goula, R. Alessandroni (model workshop)
**Landscape Architects:** Edaw, London
**Engineers:** Europroject Consultores Asociados, José María Velasco (Engineer)
**Constructor:** Benjumea

## Campus of the University of Vigo

**Architects in charge:** B.T.,Dani Rosselló, Elena Rocchi
**EMBT project collaborators:**
**Lecture room building. Execution project:** M. de Rooij, F. Massoni, L. Giovannozzi, K. Chada, A. Landell de Moura, J. Hendricks, A. M. Henao, M.A. Ávila, C. Hidalgo, S. Henriques, R. Herrin-Ferri, M. de Rosa, K. Bonhag, D. Mc Kenzie (model workshop)
**Sports area. Execution project:** R. Sforza, F. Massoni, C. Höfler, E. Nedelcu, S. Nunes Henriques, C. Hidalgo, R. De Montard, J. Krüger, S. Geenen, T. Hosie, M. Andres (model workshop)
**Campus urbanization. Execution project:** R. Sforza, F. Massoni, C. Höfler, E. Nedelcu, M. Chizzola, A. Borsetti, A. Marcela Henao, I.Quintana, J.P. Uribe (model workshop)
**Rectorates. Execution project:** Ll. Corbella, E. Nedelcu, N. Laverde, K. Bonifaz, P. Michaud, P. Sándor Nagy, S. Nunes Henriques, C. Vernier, J. Villamil, J. Krüguer, A. Quantrill, R. Fatti, D. Mayer, D. Erfeld, E. Farkas (model workshop)
**Footbridge. Execution project:** Kenneth Bonifaz, C. Vernier, J. Villamil, M. Vermeiren (model workshop).
**Shopping, cinema and theatre building. Execution project:** E. Nedelcu, K. Bonifaz, N. Laverde, P. Michaud, A. Clausen, F. Mota, S. Geenen, S. Henriques, C. Vernier.
**Campus. Basic Project:** Elena Rocchi, D. Rosselló, X. Rodríguez, R. Herrin-Ferri, Fabián Asunción (head of model workshop), L. Giovannozzi, T. Stauss, M. Lechelt, A. Höller, S. Techen, S. Stecklina, A.M. Henao (model workshop)
**Technical architects:** Manolo Cuquejo; Tecnic G3; **Structure:** IOC, Nilo Lletjós, MC2, Julio Martínez Calzón (footbridge); **Installations:** Proisotec, Josep Masachs; **Constructors:** Malvar-OHL; **Architect collaborator:** Julio Rodríguez-Daniel Rivoira (works direction); **Consultant:** CIISA, **Constructor:** UTE Puentes y Calzados SA (phase 1); NECSO (phase 2)

## Scottish Parliament

**Architects:** E.M. + B.T. in association with RMJM Scotland LTD
**Architects in charge:** E.M. + B.T., Joan Callís, Karl Unglaub
**EMBT project collaborators:**
**Execution project:** Constanza Chara, Umberto Viotto, Fergus McArdle, L. Giovannozzi, F. Matucci, E. Bottigella, T. Skoetz, E. Cirulli, A. Nasser, J. Rollán Raffin, G. Lambrechts, S. Brunner, P. Sándor Nagy
**Basic project:** M. Eichhorn, C. Chara, U. Viotto, F. McArdle, S. Belli, G. Silva Nicoletti, V. Franza, A. Benaduce, A. Vrana, B. Ríos, T. Skoetz, T. Sakamoko, J. García Germán, Fabián Asunción (head of model workshop), A.M. Henao, A. Gaspar Caspado, N. Pröwer, S. Belli, P. Ogesto Vallina, L. Giovannozzi, S. Hay, M. Santini, F. Matucci, C. Felber, M. de la Porta, S. Henriques, L. Di Romanico, J. Locke, Ch.Stauss, S. Stecklina, S. Brussaferi, C. Lucchini, S. Geenen, K. Kinder, F. Bartsh, Adam Strong, C. Molina, P. Giacobbe, R. Du Montard, F. Vechter (model workshop)
**Competition:** Joan Callis (project team); M. Eichhorn, F. Mozzati, O. Arbel, S. Bacaus, C. Chara, C. Hitz, Fabián Asunción, A. M. Henao, F. McArdle, R. Jiménez, L. Giovannozzi (model workshop)

### Restoration of Santa Caterina Market

Architects in charge: B. T., Igor Peraza, Joan Callís
EMBT project collaborators:
Execution project: Hirotaka Koizuni, Josep Miàs, T. Sakamoto, M. Cases, C. Chara, J. Poca, A. Vázquez, M. Dario, J. Belles, A. Bramon, S. Crespi, G. Grondona, L. Valentini, A. Passetti, Ll. Corbella, J. Carvajal, M. Fukuda, A. Landell de Moura, I. Zaragoza, T. Skoetz, A. Verschuere, L. Gestin, A.M. Henao, E. Cattaneo, F. Asunción, L. Giovannozzi, A. Hoëller, S. Bauchmann, S. Techen, B. Oel Brandt, M. Olsen, F. Vetcher, N. Becker, R. de Montard, M. Galindo, B. Appolloni, J. F. Vaudeville, P.S. Nagy, M. Chizzola, Fabián Asunción (head of model workshop), I.Quintana, C. Molina, M. Vermeiren, T. Schmid (model workshop)
Basic Project: Joan Callis, Makoto Fukuda, Hirotaka Kuizumi, A. Ebbeskov Olsen, D. Rosselló, F. Mozzati, F. Jacques-Dias, F. Hannah
Competition: E. Rocchi, R. Flores, G. Zambrana, Ll. Cantallops, A.M. Tosi, M. Forteza, A. Galmer, Silvia, L. Bonforte, Fabián Asunción, T. Gottschalk, S. Eckert, U. Grölz, T. Wuttke, L. Tonella, S. Le Draoullec, M. Carrera (model workshop)
Special collaboration: Ricardo Flores, Eva Prats
Structure: Robert Brufau, José María Velasco, Miquel Llorens
Installations: PGI

### Istituto Universitario di Architettura di Venezia

Architects in charge: B.T., Elena Rocchi
EMBT project collaborators:
Execution project: J. García Germán, T. Sakamoto, T. Skoetz, M. Chirdel, M. Fukuda, M. Batalla, E. Bottigella, J. Martínez, L. Valentini, G. Grondona, E. Cirulli, S. Crespi, K. Bonifaz, N. Laverde, A. Haaning, Fabián Asunción (head of model workshop), A. Henao, A. Gaspar Caspado, M. Coing Maillet, L. Giovannozzi, S. Nunes, M. De Rosa, R. de Montard, A.J. Quintana, S. Geenen, M. Zimmerhakl, J.I. Quintana (model workshop)
Basic Project: N.F. de Almeida, M. de Rooij, J. Garcia Germán, T. Sakamoto, Fabián Asunción, A.M. Henao, S. Nunes Henriques, M. De Rosa, B. Oelbrandt, R. De Montard, F. Vetcher (model workshop)
Competition phase 1: O. Arbel, M. Fukuda, H. Koizumi, T. Kappel, A. Catania, A.M. Henao, J. Grebe, C. Chara, M. Eichorn, S. Becaus, M. Coing-Maillet
Competition phase 2: M. Fukuda, E.Rocchi, A. Vrana, H. Koizumi, T. Sakomoto, A. Reiber, E. Frances, N.F. de Almeida, M. de Rooij, S. Becaus, Fabián Asunción, A.M. Henao, M Coing Maillet, A.G. Caspado, L. Giovannozzi, M. Santini, A. Charisius, R. Breit, M. Della Porta (model workshop)
Structure: Mauro Giuliani, Studio Redesco, Milan; Fire prevention: Studio Beppe Camporini, Venecia; Installations: ng, C,Pagani (executive project)
Engineering: Mc2, Estudio de Ingeniería. Ing. Julio Martínez Calzón; Coordination: Studio Beppe Camporini, Venice; Acoustics: Higini Arau (basic project)
Engineering: Ove Arup; Engineer: Steve Fischer, Ove Arup, London; Technical architect: Davide Fortarel (competition)

### Gas Natural Headquarters

Architects in charge: B.T., Elena Rocchi, Josep Ustrell
EMBT project collaborators:
Execution project: A. Moura, Ll. Corbella, R. Sforza, L. Valentini, M. Chizzola, S. Crespi, M. del Olmo, E. Nedelcu, P. S. Nagy, B. Molina, S. Geenen, M. Pierres, F. Bernal, A. Gómez, D. Erfeld, J. Rollan, M. Sánchez, A. Stoppani, D. Mayer, N. Rodrigues (model workshop)
Basic Project: Joan Callís, Lluís Cantallops, L. Giovannozzi, F. Massoni, A. Landell de Moura, E. Cirulli, R. Sforza, U. Viotto, M. Batalla, L. Petinal, R. Song, Fabián Asunción (head of model workshop), R. de Montard (model workshop)
Competition: X. Rodríguez, T. Sakamoto, J. García Germán, D. Rosselló, M. de Rooij, U. Viotto, T. Skoetz, S. Belli, J. Miàs, M. Cases, E. Cattaneo Fabián Asunción, L. Giovannozzi, F. Matucci, R. de Montard, S. Henriques, J. Löcke, C. Stauss, B. Oelbrandt, M. Olsen, J. Salhab, A. Kita, A.M. Henao (model workshop)
Structure: Julio Martínez Calzón, MC2 Estudio de Ingeniería, Madrid
Instalations: PGI Grup; Technical architects: CIC. M.Roig i Assoc. SL

### Hafencity

Competition
Architects in charge: B. T., Elena Rocchi, Karl Unglaub
EMBT project collaborators:
Competition collaborators phase 1: M. Chizzola, L. Valentini, G. Grondona, L. Ortiz, B. Minués, S. Geenen, C. Molina, N. Rodrigues, M. Pierres, J. Roldán, D. Erfeld, A. Gómez, M. Sánchez, C. Pinzón, F. Bernal
Exterior spaces. Competition collaborators phase 2: A. Pasetti, S. Geenen, N. Torres, E. Nedelcu, L. Ortiz, B. Mínguez, U. Viotto, R. Sforza, G. Grondona, J. Carvajal, F. Mota, S. Brunner, J. Rollán, E. Cirulli, S. Crespi, C. Molina, N. Rodrigues, M. Pierres, E. Farkas, J. Roldán, D. Erfeld, G. Cardone, A. Gómez, M. Sánchez, C. Pinzón, F. Bernal, D. Mayer, A. Stoppani, N. Almeida, A. Gómez Infante
Art: Thomas Bayrle
Ing. Alberto Scotti